SPA VALLEY RAILWAY

DAVID STAINES

HALSGROVE

First published in Great Britain in 2009

British Library Cataloguing-in-Publication Data
A CIP record for this title is available from the British Library

ISBN 978 1 84114 928 8

HALSGROVE
Halsgrove House,
Ryelands Industrial Estate,
Bagley Road, Wellington, Somerset TA21 9PZ
Tel: 01823 653777 Fax: 01823 216796
email: sales@halsgrove.com

Part of the Halsgrove group of companies
Information on all Halsgrove titles is available at: www.halsgrove.com

Printed and bound by Grafiche Flaminia, Italy

INTRODUCTION

On 6th July 1985 the shadows of a glorious mid-summer evening started to lengthen. Standing in the fields high on the hillside between High Rocks and Groombridge the Wealden countryside was visible for miles. In the valley below the distinctive oast-houses at Pokehill caught the very last rays of the sun. The sound of a diesel train, working up the gradient out of Groombridge caught the distant air. Soon it emerged from the trees and slowly passed through the landscape. It was a timeless scene, yet that very evening the railway's time was over. This was the day that British Rail closed the railway. After a century of service it only had a few hours left to carry its last passengers. The scrap man would take the rails, the sleepers would be burnt and nature would take back the cuttings and embankments.

Twenty years to the day, on 6th July 2005 I returned to exactly the same spot. Little in the landscape had changed. A few trees had grown noticeably taller and the farm had been spruced up from its previous ramshackle state. With the shadows again lengthening at precisely the same time an identical sound could be heard in the distance and before long a diesel train again passed slowly by. It was even the very same train. The intervening two decades had seen a long, heroic and hard-fought battle to bring the railway back from the dead. The clock had been put back and the railway restored and established not only as a living heritage transport link serving both the community and famous visitor attractions along its course, but also making an important contribution to the local economy. This is the Spa Valley Railway. In comparison to other heritage railways it is a 'late arrival'. However such youthfulness also pays dividends; the railway's volunteer base is on average younger than most and its use of both steam and heritage diesel traction appeals to visitors across the generations.

This volume covers the twenty five years from 1983 to 2008 taking you on a pictorial journey back to the struggle to save the line and then along the length of the railway showcasing the contrasting scenes, beautiful landscape and variety of locomotives and rolling stock which make the Spa Valley one of the most popular and diverse heritage railways in the South East. The book concludes with the dawn of the next chapter in the railway's life – to be covered in a subsequent volume – a groundbreaking project, unprecedented in its complexity, with trains sharing National Rail infrastructure for nearly a mile of railway into Eridge station.

When compiling a volume such this, I must acknowledge the many people who have supported the book and my thanks go to everyone who has assisted in a whole variety of ways, from answering enquiries to facilitating rolling stock movements for photography. My particular thanks go to Jon & Chris Nye, Matt Dives and Vicky & Darren Skinner. Similarly it could not have been completed without the support, assistance and interest shown by my wife Hilary and daughter Katie.

David Staines.

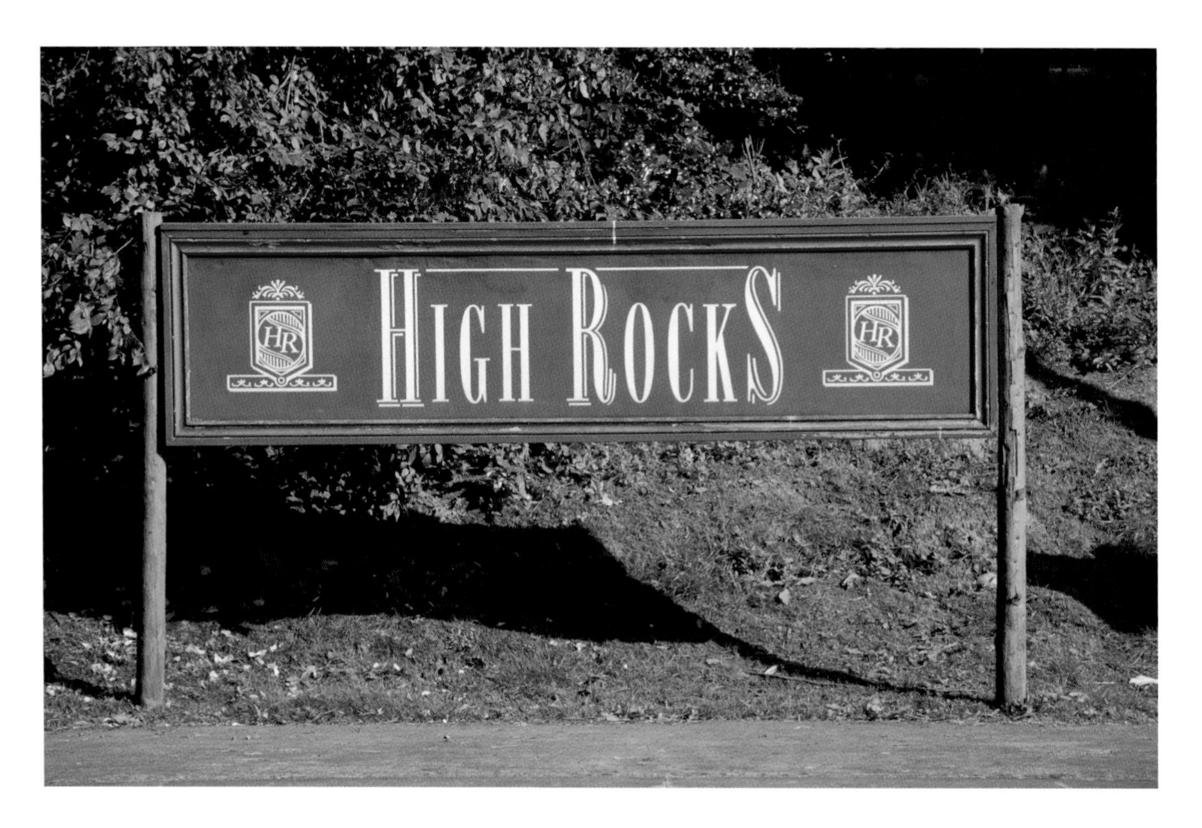

HISTORICAL BACKGROUND

When the railway came to Tunbridge Wells the town was provided with two main-line stations provided by competing companies. Tunbridge Wells Central was opened by the South Eastern Railway in 1852 and Tunbridge Wells West by the London, Brighton and South Coast in 1866, the latter the terminus of a cross-country route from East Grinstead via Groombridge. This section forms part of today's Spa Valley Railway. A patchwork building of new railways saw the development of a complex and now partly forgotten rural system. In 1868 the line from Groombridge Junction to Uckfield was opened, the stretch as far as Eridge now the other part of the Spa Valley. By the end of the nineteenth century Tunbridge Wells West was the hub of this network of lines, the station dispatching trains to destinations in five separate directions. It was so busy that new infrastructure was needed and 1891 saw the construction of the locomotive shed that is the headquarters of today's Spa Valley Railway. At High Rocks a halt was opened in 1906 and lasted until 1952.

The 1950s saw the network spiral into decline. Despite the introduction of new diesels, in 1963 BR proposed the first local line closure and by 1966 wished to close the entire local network west of the Hastings line at Tunbridge Wells. Vigorous protests saw Oxted–Uckfield and Tunbridge Wells–Eridge survive. The Eridge line hung on, but by 1982 British Rail was again seeking closure, claiming £¾ million would be required to upgrade the infrastructure, and that despite carrying 200,000 passengers a year, the expenditure could not be justified. Certainly no money had been invested in the line for years. Even by the early 1980s it was a virtual museum of bygone railway operating practice. At Tunbridge Wells West there were still two signal boxes controlling an impressive array of semaphore signals whilst the booking hall still enjoyed faint illumination by gas lights! At Eridge, again controlled by semaphore signals, trains had to shunt from one side of the station to the other between arrival and departure. Despite protests, 6th July 1985 saw the last passenger trains run, the last run of all being the 23.10 Uckfield–Tunbridge Wells West. However a determined group of people refused to allow the railway to die…

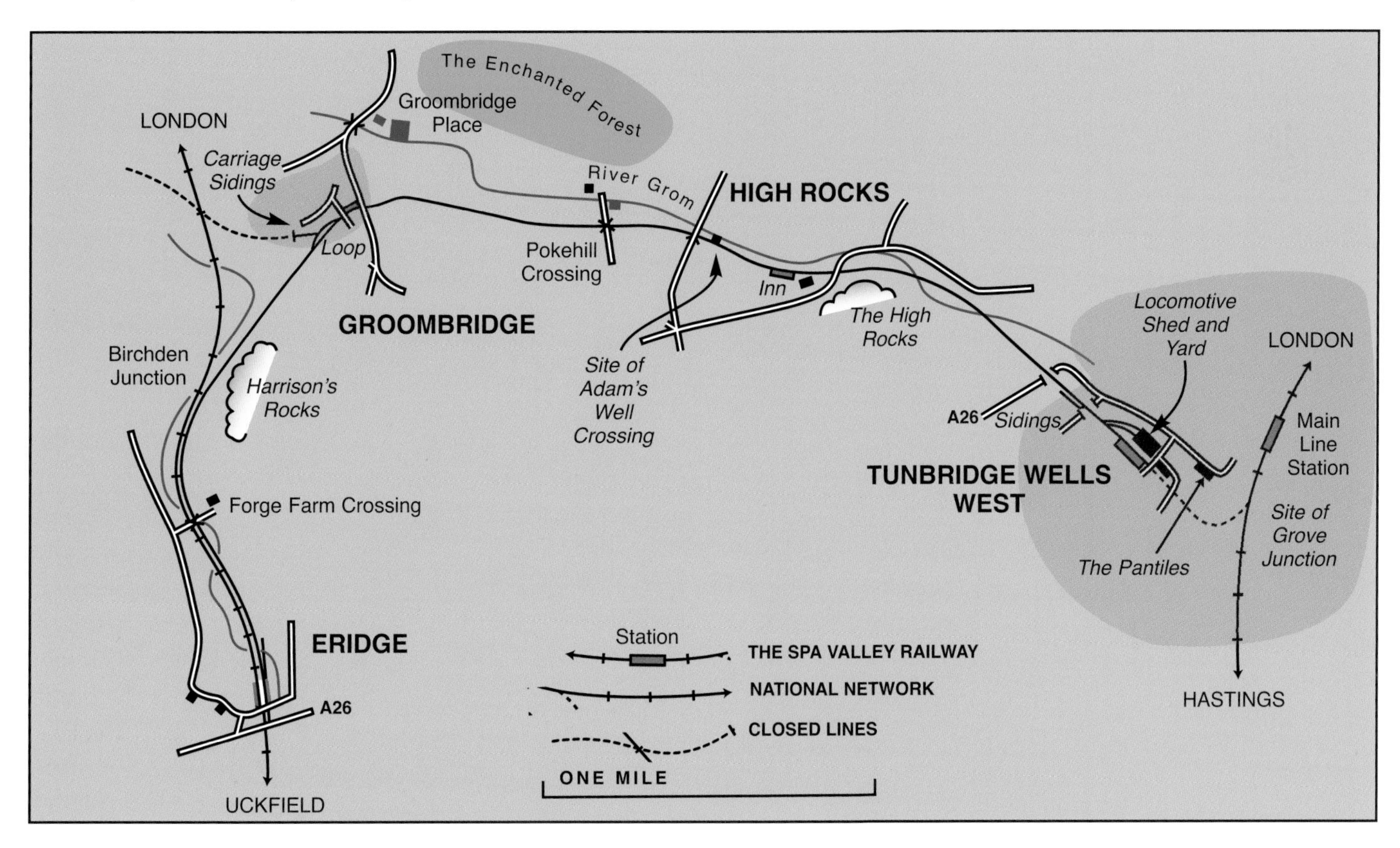

The Early Years

The final years as part of the British Rail system. With closure on the horizon there is no expenditure on modernisation. Like the rest of the railway Birchden Junction maintains a whole host of traditional railway features with some fascinating details, right down to the carefully cut back grass and logs stacked at the apex of the junction. On 26th March 1983, shortly after BR announced their final intention to close the railway, Class 207 1302 forms a Tonbridge–Eridge service on what is now the Spa Valley line.

What was to become the Spa Valley Railway had only one day left as a passenger carrying line for British Railways when this picture was taken of the old booking hall at Tunbridge Wells West on 5th July 1985. To mark the passing of the railway a plywood coffin and wreath stand next to the formal notice of closure, the scene still illuminated by gas light.

The last day at Groombridge. Class 207 diesel units 1317 and 1311 are full of enthusiasts enjoying a final ride. Amid the spectators on the platform a lady with a suitcase and accompanying dog show that even on the day the railway closed, it was still an important transport link for local people. Unit 1317 was to make a proud return to the railway twenty years later.

A glorious midsummer evening as the sun sets on the 'last day'. Units 1317 and 1311 form the 19.59 Eridge–Tunbridge Wells Central past Pokehill Farm. Although unforeseen at the time, Pokehill's oast houses were set to feature prominently in photography during the following years, although the environment of the farm has changed significantly since 1985.

After closure to passengers, the line remained open until 10th August for the passage of empty trains to and from the depot at Tunbridge Wells West. On 29th July BR despatched what would be their very last locomotive to Tunbridge Wells West, sending 33061 on a works train to recover redundant fuel storage tanks for reuse at New Cross Gate.

A pressure group set up to challenge the closure decision was unsuccessful in the High Court. However, this set the seeds of revival. A month after closure, public meetings were held introducing the concept of a revived single track operation, based in the locomotive shed at Tunbridge Wells West. This is the view from 'B' signal box in November 1985. All of the land in the foreground is occupied today by retail stores and car parks.

Objectors to a pre-existing draft 'local plan' which had left no room for the railway at the West station, forced a public enquiry. This concluded that the site offered a unique opportunity for the railway to reopen with the locomotive shed being placed in a conservation area. Ultimately, Sainsbury's plan for the site included generous provision for the retention of the railway around the shed, which had last been used in 1978.
In this October 1988 photograph, on the right hand side volunteers make a start on clearing away ten years of vegetation from the area which is now the centre of the railway's operations. The right hand side of the platform is roughly the site of its counterpart today.

June 1988 was probably the darkest hour for the preservation society. British Rail wished to remove the junction at Birchden. Although they saw less urgency in recovering the track back to Tunbridge Wells, they considered the most cost effective way to do this was by rail. Therefore, the entire railway would have to be pulled up before the junction was taken out. The society was given eight weeks to put down a substantial deposit. On 12th July a deposit of £40,000 was offered. A lease was taken out on the ground floor of Groombridge Station, seen slumbering on 23rd October 1988, where the railway's first headquarters and shop were established.

Left

The setting sun illuminates a scene of dereliction inside the locomotive shed on 27th November 1988. Smoke from burning sleepers hangs in the air outside. The transformation to today's thriving headquarters could hardly be more marked.

Above

Debris from track removal litters the Tunbridge Wells site, seen from Broadwater Lane Bridge on 29th January 1989. In due course, Sainsbury's building contractor assisted the society with heavy engineering work in return for 56 weeks' tenure of the back of the loco shed for use as site offices. Excepting the shed area on the left of the picture, the rest of the land would be redeveloped for retail use.

Permission was given for some material to be salvaged from the Tunbridge Wells West site and redundant sleepers, points and rails were recovered for reuse. On 26th March 1989, platform coping stones are being salvaged. Three years of neglect have taken their toll on the main station buildings.

In 1987 the society had purchased its first locomotive, a small 153hp diesel shunter built by Drewry in 1959 and it was moved to the Lavender Line for storage. In order for the railway to have a presence at the opening of the Sainsbury's Superstore in 1990, it was decided that a short length of temporary track would be relaid adjacent to the newly built platform and the public would be given demonstration rides. With the shunter needing to be moved by road from Isfield to Eridge, a diversion via Tunbridge Wells was possible. On 20th August an incredible 660 people enjoyed a cab ride. The Drewry is lowered by crane, becoming the first locomotive to arrive on the railway in preservation.

The Drewry shunter was moved, again by road, to Eridge and is here seen running on the long down siding on 25th November 1990.

British Rail had lodged a planning application for the station site at Groombridge which would cut the railway in half. Following 300 letters of objection, the application was amended to preserve a 'right of way' for the railway. In March 1989, a licence was granted to the society to occupy the railway in the Groombridge area in order to commence track work changes to accommodate the proposed housing development. This June 1992 view sees a juxtaposition of old and new. The foundations for the first building of the new housing estate are already taking shape before the rest of the site is cleared away.

Given the loss of the original site, a new platform at Groombridge in the cutting to the south of the former station area was built and paid for by the developers. In this picture of 27th June 1992 all looks quiet. Behind the scenes, the month saw the granting of a Light Railway Order by the Secretary of State for Transport. Ultimately, purchase of the railway was achieved after BR halved the asking price and Tunbridge Wells Borough Council offered significant financial assistance in the form of a grant and long loan.

Spring 1996 saw the finalisation of the purchase of the railway from Broadwater Lane Bridge to Birchden Junction. On 1st February work is taking place at Groombridge to create a run round loop out of the former double track in the cutting.

Above

Also in Spring 1996, the arrival of rolling stock was greatly accelerated by the decision of the North Downs Steam Railway to relocate from Stone near Dartford to the Spa Valley. Most of their assets were transported to Tunbridge Wells. This necessitated rapid reinstatement of the track in the locomotive shed and yard. New arrivals are seen on 20th April.

Right

21st December saw a moment of crowning glory – the first public trains. The railway inspectorate granted permission for the first three quarter mile of line to be reopened as far as Coldbath Bridge. Despite the best attempts of the weather, eight days over the Christmas and New Year period saw 2,500 passengers carried. 28th December was the only decent day for photography and '*North Downs*', built in 1955 by Robert Stephenson & Hawthorn is seen pounding up the last few yards into Tunbridge Wells West.

23rd August 1997 saw the extension of services to Groombridge. Again '*North Downs*' was in charge and is seen running into the platform with the very first public train from Groombridge to Tunbridge Wells in preservation.

On 13th April 1998 beautiful evening light sees Barclay *'Lady Ingrid'*, the next steam locomotive to enter service on the railway, drift into the new platform at Groombridge.

Left

With the High Rocks Inn undergoing refurbishment and upgrading, its owner financed the reinstatement of the adjacent halt. The new platform was built to the west of the original but conveniently located at the edge of the inn's landscaped grounds. It was opened with due ceremony on 29th August 1998. On that day '*Lady Ingrid*' arrives, the wheelbarrow on the platform providing evidence of some last minute tidying up.

Above

A ceremonial 'first train' to High Rocks is flagged off by a local MP. This was also the first time the railway managed to run a double-headed passenger train, quite an achievement in the early days. Peckett '*Fonmon*' leads '*Lady Ingrid*'.

Tunbridge Wells to Groombridge

Left

The locomotive shed is now the thriving hub of the railway. It was built in 1891 with much of it constructed on top of massive brick arches, unseen beneath the floor today, in exactly the same way used to support many of the big terminal stations in London. This is one of just a handful of Victorian locomotive sheds in the whole country still serving their original purpose.

Above

During an air raid in the Second World War the shed received a direct hit; the bomb went through the roof, pierced the floor and ended up in the arches beneath. Amazingly it failed to explode although it still caused major damage to the roof which was not replaced until the 1950s. '*Lady Ingrid*' faces the low winter sunshine illuminating the inside of the shed.

68077

Left

Showing signs of outside storage at its previous home, London & North Eastern Railway 'J94' 68077 arrived on the railway on Christmas Eve 2005 and is seen safely in the shed shortly after. BR closed the shed in 1965 when steam was finally ousted by diesels, although from 1971 until 1978 it contained a mysterious set of coaches said to have been kept for use as an emergency strategic control train in case of nuclear war.

Above

The rear wall of the shed, which a locomotive is said to have once ploughed through and out the other side, is now a convenient place to hang locomotive headboards awaiting repeat use.

Left
The shed is also the preserve of traditional engineering skills being learnt and re-learnt and passed from generation to generation. Here boiler tubes are being replaced.
Right
At the other end of the spectrum the dry environment is vital when painting locomotives and rolling stock. The finishing touch – the famous British Rail double arrow emblem – is applied to Class 73 E6047.

Above

All in a day's work – the patient task of oiling around, preparing *'Lady Ingrid'* for a day's duty on the railway...

Right

...whilst at the end of the day one of the less glamorous, but necessary aspects of driving a steam locomotive is disposal. Ash is shovelled from *'Lady Ingrid'*s smoke box.

Left
In near silhouette, the driver and fireman of Peckett *'Fonmon'* are caught in conversation.

Proving that photography can be an all weather exercise. The rain lashes down on E6047 as it stands outside the shed in during a downpour. An ordinary yet timeless scene.

On the same evening the monsoon like rain is creeping underneath the shed doors as, safe inside, *'Spartan'* nears the end of an overhaul.

Former London and South Western Railway 1874 vintage well tank 30587 visited the railway in 2007. With its driver keeping a watchful eye the locomotive (part of the National Railway Museum collection) moves off the shed.

Another 2007 visitor was the Bluebell Railway's E4 32473 '*Birch Grove*', a locomotive which would have been a familiar visitor to Tunbridge Wells in steam days. In a wonderfully atmospheric scene steam is raised in the shed and hangs in the air on a cold morning.

Just in case…once familiar 'furniture' on the railways, but now a sight from the past.
A trio of fire buckets hang on the shed wall.

Somewhat out of context, this vintage sign is next to the foot crossing outside the front doors to the locomotive shed.

Driving wheels from a steam locomotive under repair make a curious sight bunched together in the yard.

'You have been warned'.

63
6583

Left
Freshly painted in BR blue livery 33063 (bearing its former number 6583) stands in the shed yard shortly after arrival on the railway. Built by the Birmingham Railway Carriage and Wagon Company it entered service in 1962.
Right
Details of the works plate of '*Fonmon*' caught by the setting sun.

Snapshots...The camaraderie of both volunteers and locomotive-owning groups is a vital ingredient to the well being of a preserved railway. The Spa Valley is fortunate in being one of the friendliest heritage railways in the country.

Right

Members of the South East Locomotive Group celebrate the naming of Class 33 33063 *'RJ Mitchell'* in honour of the designer of the legendary Spitfire aircraft.

Above

Volunteers salute one of the railway's most unusual visitors: Aveling & Porter *'Blue Circle'* after it has undertaken the longest passenger carrying journey of its career. (See also page 71)

75F
65
REMEMBERED

Class 10 diesel shunter D3489 *'Colonel Tomline'* awaits its next duty. The top half of the signal box in the background was originally at Buckden in Cambridgeshire where it had been built by the Midland Railway. After the railway closed there it was used as a greenhouse. Unfortunately arson attacks in the late 1980s rendered both of the original signal boxes at Tunbridge Wells West unfit for further use.

Above

Built by RSH in 1950 as their works No 7673, '*Ugly*' stands outside the shed. The roller shutter doors are a recent addition, vital to ensure the security of the shed.

Right

A small but attractive station garden between the platform and shed yard brightens the aspect for waiting passengers.

'Lady Ingrid' is the only locomotive to display the railway's crest. Here she is running round her train on a crisp winter's day. The buffer stops mark the eastern limit of the railway.

One of a handful of industrial shunters occasionally used on the railway, *'Princess Margaret'*, built by Barclay in 1949, ticks over in the yard. Behind it *'Topham'* has had its boiler removed for overhaul.

D
6695

Left

Former Great Western Railway 'Taffy Tank' 6695 stands in the new platform at Tunbridge Wells West. Looking beyond the buffer stops, the 'Old West Station' restaurant was originally the main station building. Now isolated from the tracks it is a Grade II listed building. Built in a grand gothic style in 1866 it was designed to impress, reputedly the architecture was based on Calais Town Hall!

Above

It's not all oil, grease and coal dust. The railway frequently plays host to wedding parties, usually in connection with functions at High Rocks. The happy couple pose next to Ex London Midland and Scottish Railway 'Jinty' 47493 which has been decked out for the occasion.

1
PERCY

Whilst controversial to the die-hard railway enthusiast, children's theme days are an important part of the railway's calendar and introduce many youngsters to a railway for the first time.

Left

'*Blue Circle*', visiting 'Jinty' 47327 and '*Fonmon*' are adorned with locomotive faces for a 'Day out with Thomas' event.

Above

'Jinty' 47327 appears to be having difficulty with some 'troublesome trucks'.

Standing next to the locomotive shed at the visitors' entrance to the site is BR Mark 1 TSORB No.S69306, formerly part of electric multiple unit No.7036. Built at York in 1965, for many years this has served as the railway's stationary buffet.

Two ex-BR locomotives together in the platform at Tunbridge Wells West. 32650 '*Sutton*' is on display as 'Jinty' 47493 arrives with a service train. '*Sutton*' was the first ex-London Brighton & South Coast Railway locomotive to take up residence in the ex LB&SCR locomotive shed since the end of BR steam.

Class 115 dmu 51669 stands at Tunbridge Wells West. Although not indigenous to the area, a handful of dmu vehicles are located on the railway. This vehicle was built at Derby in 1960.

Swedish 'SJ' Class locomotive No 1928 spent several years on the railway. Unlike most other locomotives it was never part of the Spa Valley's fleet, its owners merely using the line as a storage and restoration site. It is standing in an area known as the East-West Sidings beyond Broadwater Lane Bridge.

A rare sight as the low autumn sunshine catches all three of the railway's 350hp diesel shunters hauling a train past the East-West Sidings into Tunbridge Wells during a 2003 gala. In order of appearance up the hill they are 15224, D3489 and 09004.

'*Sutton*' is owned by the London Borough of Sutton and owes its survival to an unusual turn of events. In 1963, recognising the importance the railway played in that borough's development, the 1876 veteran was bought for static display as the centrepiece of a new civic centre. At that time, the plans were still only on the drawing board and the locomotive was still in working order. It was given a temporary home on the Kent and East Sussex Railway where it was anticipated it would see short term use before being 'stuffed and mounted' as a static museum piece.
Ultimately the plans changed and the locomotive saw considerable use on the K&ESR. After a lengthy period out of use, the borough agreed to move the engine to Tunbridge Wells for restoration and use on the Spa Valley. Shortly after arrival, in April 2004 '*Sutton*' is decked out with discs and lamps and posed for photographs outside Tunbridge Wells.

Rarities on the line include the Metropolitan Railway T stock vehicles 2749 and 2758. These were built in 1932 as part of six car electric sets for Metropolitan Railway services from Baker Street and survived withdrawal in the 1960s when converted to a de-icing unit.

After leaving Tunbridge Wells, the line runs on an embankment past Ramslye. Galas usually feature trains running into the late evening which in summer also affords the rare opportunity of sunlit pictures on the northern side of the line. 73140 & 33065 top and tail one such train with 37254 on the rear.

Hiring out whole trains or individual carriages for birthdays or other celebrations is a useful source of income. Carrying suitable headboards, 37254 is seen on one such evening working as the sun sets on the long straight between Ramslye and Coldbath Bridge.

Away from Tunbridge Wells, the railway runs on a descending gradient, initially as steep as 1 in 88. In this area, mostly designated as ancient semi-natural woodland, 73140 and 6583 are seen reforming a complex engineer's working.

Back in 2000, nature seemed quite keen on reclaiming the railway. *'Fonmon'* leads a demonstration goods away from High Rocks during the May Steam Gala of that year. *'Fonmon'* was built in 1924 by Peckett of Bristol and spent its working life in South Wales.

A Great Western double. GW-built 'Taffy Tank' 6695 is banked by GW-designed 9466 through Friezland Woods.

Although now eclipsed by larger locomotives, the Drewry shunter still sees occasional trips down the line. Here it is moving empty coaching stock between Coldbath Bridge and High Rocks.

On 28th March 2008 37254 and 33063 top and tail an engineers' train on the approach to High Rocks. 37254 had only arrived on the railway the day beforehand following extensive restoration at a private site near Ashford, where it had been limited to a run of a few track panels. This was the first train the locomotive had worked in over nine years.

High Rocks to Groombridge

Left

Class 25 D7612 approaches High Rocks with an evening 'Real Ale Train'. The original High Rocks Halt was open from 1907–1952 apart from a short break during the Second World War. The up platform stood in the foreground, accessed by a short footpath from the lane on the left.

Above

Polish TKh locomotive 2944 '*Hotspur*' approaches High Rocks. The location takes its name from the adjacent 5 million year old Ardingly Sandstone outcrops, now designated a site of special scientific importance. Carbon dating of artefacts has proved man lived here 4000 years ago, one of the earliest proven locations of human habitation in the entire country.

Left
The rocks themselves provide an excellent vantage point for photography. 33065 passes with an up train. In the background the converted oast houses at High Rocks Farm are now a private residence.

Right
One of the most unusual visitors to the railway was Aveling & Porter '*Blue Circle*'. By their very nature this type of locomotive led a very restricted existence. However on the evening of 28th April 2007 it was attached to the 'Queen Mary' brake van and took a small party of Spa Valley volunteers down the line from Tunbridge Wells to High Rocks and back. In its entire life it was the furthest distance the locomotive had travelled conveying passengers.

PINES
EXPRESS

Above

Class 73 E6047, fresh from repaint, is posed next to the rocks which can be seen looming above the railway on the left hand side.

Right

The densely wooded nature of this part of the Kentish Weald is apparent in this view of passing 33065. Today woodland accounts for 24% of the local area compared with a 9% national average.

E4 32473 runs beneath the rocks. This area has become known as 'Tea Garden Lane' after the road heading off from the triangle towards the farm. The temptation to digitally remove the distracting parked car was (just) overcome!

'Lady Ingrid' battles the gradient away from the new platform seen through High Rocks Lane Bridge.

Great Western Railway Pannier Tank 7715 passes beneath High Rocks Lane and past the site, on the right, of the former up platform. After withdrawal by BR 7715 was bought by London Transport for further use on the surface lines of the London underground network.

33063 propels the 'Queen Mary' brake van and part restored Class 101 dmu driving trailer 54408 into High Rocks. The unusual combination is passing the site of the original down platform. The metal supports for the top of a flight of stairs which used to drop down from the lane to the platform can still be seen embedded in the masonry of the bridge.

The piecemeal building of what is now the Spa Valley Railway provides a baffling legacy of mileposts. This is mp 48 ¼ at High Rocks – but it is only 37 miles from London via Tonbridge. However railways usually remain measured according to the historical first route to open, and that was the longer route from London via Three Bridges which closed in 1966. The section from Birchden Junction to Groombridge similarly remains measured from Brighton (mp 28 is at Birchden). After 1985 BR took the unusual step of changing the remaining Uckfield line mileposts to reflect the direct mileage from London via Ashurst, so the line south of Birchden Junction is now measured differently again, with mp 35 at Eridge!

GWR Pannier Tank 7715 steams into High Rocks past the smart reproduction lamp posts and manicured flower beds, watched by a young spectator.

LMS 'Jinty' 47493 waits at the new High Rocks Halt. The landscaped grounds of the inn sweep down towards the platform. The observant will notice the locomotive is facing 'chimney first' down the valley. 47493 spent only a few months facing this way between two visits away from the railway in 2005.

The railway won an award for its conversion of a standard Mark I corridor coach into luxury bar car '*Kate*'. Lunch is served as passengers await departure from High Rocks.

1317
31
1866 THE 1985
GROOMBRIDGE LINE
FAREWELL
31
SQUADRON
SAVE
THE
ERIDGE
LINE
SAVE
THE
ERIDGE
LINE

Left
In 2005 two coaches of demu 1317, the train that had formed most services on the day the railway closed to passengers 20 years beforehand, were obtained from Porterbrook leasing for a nominal sum. The original headboards carried were also located. In order to drum up some publicity for an event marking the passage of two decades since closure a re-enactment of the accompanying closure protests was also created.

Right
Built by BR at Darlington in 1958, Class 10 No D3489 was obtained from the Felixstowe Dock and Harbour Board and already carried the name '*Colonel Tomline*' in honour of one of the dock's founders. In November 2001, shortly after delivery it stands amid autumn colours at High Rocks still wearing the garish livery of its former owner.

Above

After High Rocks the train soon passes through the cutting at Adams Well. A lane once crossed the line here complete with signal box and railway-built house. It is thought the old lane was originally part of the Roman Ermine Street, where once Roman legions and later King Harold's Saxon army marched to defeat at Hastings in 1066. The crossing was closed by BR back in 1958 and the public right of way was extinguished, causing so much uproar with the horse riding community that the matter was raised in both Houses of Parliament. The signal box disappeared soon after whilst the house was demolished and replaced by the current structure in the 1990s. D3489 *'Colonel Tomline'* is seen again, now restored to a more sombre BR black livery.

Right

'Lady Ingrid' makes an assault on the gradient through the cutting. These April photographs show the Spa Valley's passengers can admire a stunning carpet of spring-time bluebells to rival any other line – names not withstanding!

Above
At Pokehill the woodland thins out and disappears as the railway has now descended to the bottom of the valley of the River Grom. The visit of 1954-built 2-6-4T standard tank 80078 in 2004 was noteworthy as this was the first occasion that a locomotive of a type used by BR in steam days had returned to the line. Seen at Pokehill on 18th September, it makes light work of its four-coach load.

Above right
The repainting of 73140 into early BR blue became quite a protracted affair. As a result it ran for much of 2004 in bright blue undercoat. The garish apparition is seen lifting its train away from Pokehill crossing.

Right
Their exhaust seemingly merging with the scudding clouds, '*Lady Ingrid*' and '*Fonmon*' tackle the gradient back towards Tunbridge Wells.

35
W

This more open stretch of line is a favourite area for photographs with some markedly contrasting forms of motive power recorded over the years. In the early days there was usually only one operable steam locomotive available on any given occasion, before the arrival of the ex-BR diesels. On 18th October 1997 the failure of the day's booked loco provided the rare sight of tiny 1957 built Ruston & Hornsby four wheel shunter *'Scottie'* pressed into service hauling a single coach from the Metropolitan Railway T stock set.

Six years later and things are very different. Late shunting at Tunbridge Wells at the start of the 2004 'Mixed Traction Gala' saw locomotives out of position to take up their allotted diagrams. The solution was to send out the 10.30 departure treble headed with three ex-BR main line locomotives. 33065, 33063 and 80078 pass Pokehill.

The Spa Valley's annual August Diesel Gala is a major event in the heritage diesel calendar and frequently a visiting locomotive is hired in as an added attraction. The 2006 event saw Class 20 20118 *'Saltburn-by-the-Sea'* attend from the South Devon Railway. In somewhat garish BR 'red stripe railfreight' livery it passes Pokehill.

Working hard '*Fonmon*' leaves a volcanic trail of steam over the valley. The traditional farmhouse glimpsed through the steam has since been demolished and replaced by a modern structure.

Above

Polish TKh 3144 '*Spartan*' lays another curtain of steam across the valley, this time heading downhill towards Groombridge. Note the Southern Railway permanent way hut, a precast design found across the entire south of England.

Right

'Jinty' 47493 is caught in a lucky patch of sunlight. Pokehill's oast houses nestle beneath the steep ridge of the hill behind. At one time all the fields hereabouts were given over to hop production. The name 'Poke' means a sack containing 8–10 bushels of green hops.

47493

The most powerful locomotive ever seen on the Spa Valley – 2700hp Class 50 50019 '*Ramilies*' only ever made one journey on the line. Having been part restored at Eridge it gained special dispensation to move up to Tunbridge Wells prior to reopening of the line throughout. It was the last stock movement from beyond Birchden Junction for 10 years. The movement was required as the locomotive was leaving the railway and the only road transhipment point was at the Tunbridge Wells end of the line. The historic trip was also the first time 50019 had worked a train in preservation. It is hauling two vans, one is the property of the loco's owning group containing spares, the other was the last Spa Valley vehicle to have been stored at Eridge which required movement to a safer location.

A further contrast in motive power at Pokehill – on a Sunday evening after the end of passenger services '*Fonmon*' is utilised to haul a short engineers' train in order to place it in the correct position for midweek working parties.

There is still a hint of morning mist as Class 12 15224 brings a ballast working down the valley past Pokehill. 15224 was built to a Bullied design at Ashford in 1949, a clear precursor of the BR standard 350hp shunter. The Class 12 also featured Bullied 'boxpox' wheels and a maximum speed of 27 ½ mph for trip working.

The eclectic variety of the Spa Valley's goods stock is apparent in this view of 'Jinty' 47493 bringing a demonstration freight over the level crossing at Pokehill.

The top of the ridge of hills behind Poke's Farm provides one of the most distinctive vantage points for pictures of the railway. Unfortunately the opportunity for sunny photography is only possible late on summer evenings when the sun creeps round to the north west side of the line. '*Fonmon*' takes a goods train through the magnificent Wealden scenery.

Class 25 D7612 and Class 73 E6047 top and tail an evening train. In May 1950 the *Railway Magazine* reported '*Many of the lesser known lines of the former LB&SCR in Sussex pass through country which is picturesque in the extreme and the 30 miles from Tunbridge Wells to Eastbourne are certainly no exception*'. Today's Spa Valley is part of that line and runs in its entirety through an area designated by the government as the High Weald Area of Outstanding Natural Beauty. The designation was confirmed in 1983, and is the largest AONB in South East England.

Beyond Pokehill the railway approaches Groombridge along a straight length of line past Lealands, named after an adjacent house. As part of the scheme to convert the run round loop at Groombridge into a fully-signalled passing facility the new down outer distant signal awaits commissioning as 'Jinty' 47493 passes. Evidence of imminent track renewal is also visible.

Class 33 6583 brings an engineers' crane past Lealands. A prize find deep in the undergrowth here was a complete signal arm, discarded when BR dispensed with signalling at Groombridge in the late 1960s.

Seasonal changes at Lealands – a wonderful recreation of a 'Southern' train, all be it not prototypical. L& SWR Beattie well tank 30587 pilots LB&SCR 32473 past what in summer are flower-strewn meadows.

The rare combination of snow on the ground and blue skies finds '*Fonmon*' passing the same spot with a 'Santa Special'. Snow on the top of the carriages indicates this was the first trip of the day.

33065 opens up with a single 'Queen Mary' brake van in tow. For some years there was a permanent way restriction in place at Lealands until the track was relaid in 2008. Another view putting the railway in the context of the Wealden scenery.

'Birch Grove' pilots 'Jinty' 47493 approaching the cattle creep at Lealands. Another post for the Groombridge signalling scheme is in place.

Groombridge to Eridge

Above
The original station buildings at Groombridge remain on a short length of platform now regrettably divorced from the railway. Even the 1970s' platform lights are now a curiosity.
Right
1875 built LB&SCR 'Terrier' 662 '*Martello*' has plenty of steam to spare as it passes beneath Station Road Bridge into the new platform. Reinforcement of this bridge was undertaken by BR as part of the transfer of the railway to the preservation society.

No
562

With just a haze of exhaust from the locomotives, passengers throng the Groombridge platform on a hot May 2001 evening as *'Fonmon'* and *'Spartan'* roll in. The shed in the foreground was the temporary ticket office prior to completion of more permanent facilities.

A winter contrast – the cold air accentuates the steam generated by 1952-built Polish TKh No 2944 '*Hotspur*'. On this day two coaches were deemed sufficient to cater for out of season passenger loadings.

09004 arrives at Groombridge. Work is proceeding on the first of the canopies which now stand on either side of the station building. Another variant of the standard 350hp diesel shunter, 09004 was built by BR at Darlington in 1958.

'*Fonmon*' and '*Spartan*' arrive having just passed the original 1866 station building, the roof of which is visible behind Station Road Bridge. The station is well placed in the village and only a short walk to historic seventeenth-century Groombridge Place and its award-winning formal gardens and 'enchanted forest'.

Cameos at Groombridge. As the train coasts into the platform two mugs of staple railway refreshment, strong hot tea, are brought out for the driver and fireman…

…as morris dancers, having given a performance in the village, catch the train back to Tunbridge Wells…

…whilst at the end of the day the lamps are lit. Hopefully the wet weather is not dampening the celebrations as GWR 7715 waits at Groombridge in pouring rain with a 'Birthday Special'.

BIRTHDAY SPECIAL
7715

Left
Polish TKh '*Spartan*' is wreathed in steam before an admiring crowd. Built in 1954 and imported into the UK in 1997, it was the first locomotive to be completely rebuilt on the railway.
Above
Class 25 D7612 runs into Groombridge beneath the first of the completed station canopies. The painted advertisement on the adjacent house provides another hint of a vanished way of life.

New build with old materials. The new canopies are supported by cast iron columns and brackets of London, Chatham and Dover Railway origin having been reclaimed from the remains of Gravesend West Street Station.

The signal box takes shape at the end of the platform. The green metalwork is the lower half of the frame recovered from Birchden Junction box and is stamped 'LB&SCR'. The wooden beams mark what is now floor level.

Right
Beattie Well Tank 30587 stands at the end of the new platform extension which now incorporates the new signal box.

30587

6th July 2005 – 20 years to the night after the railway closed to passengers demu 1317, reunited with the headboards it wore two decades earlier, forms the 22.00 Groombridge–Tunbridge Wells West. Unfortunately it is not departing from the original station!

'Jinty' 47493 stunts a demonstration goods train beneath Back Lane Bridge. In the Groombridge area there are three overbridges all in close proximity. Two of them (Back Lane and School Lane) have seen extensive repairs undertaken as part of the railway's obligations to maintain public rights of way.

Although a Hawksworth GWR design, Pannier Tank 9466 was a BR product built in 1952. A frequent visitor to the railway, it stands in the cutting having run round its train.

32473

Left
Crisp early morning sunshine dapples into the cutting beyond the station as 32473 '*Birch Grove*' brings a perfect recreation of a Southern Region parcels train into the loop.
Right
Enveloped by steam, the driver and fireman of 'Terrier' 662 '*Martello*' keep a watch whilst shunting at Groombridge.

80078

Left
BR standard tank 80078 stands beneath School Lane Bridge. School Lane is known as the 'upside down' bridge as the steps on either side drop down into the cutting, unlike most bridges where the steps take pedestrians up and over the railway. It is reputed that the bridge was originally a conventional one and was put up at Battersea in South London. It is said to have been later moved to Groombridge and turned upside down to fit the cutting. The walkway is certainly much wider than it needs to be for a country path suggesting that a previously busy urban use was likely.

Right
At the end of the loop, beneath School Lane Bridge is the site of Groombridge Junction. Tracks still diverge to the right, but only for a short distance onto private land and are used as carriage sidings. The line once extended to Ashurst Junction, providing a direct link to London via Oxted, and to East Grinstead. In this view nearly all the carriages are multiple unit stock of various ages and pedigrees.

Left
'Jinty' 47493 runs round its train at a time before the loop at Groombridge was used as a passing place. 47493 was built for the London Midland and Scottish Railway by the Vulcan Foundry at Newton-le-Willows in Lancashire in 1927. It came to Tunbridge Wells West in 2000; it was then extensively overhauled and returned to traffic in 2004.

Right
The few last hundred yards of the former up line beyond Groombridge Junction have been retained as an engineers' siding. In reality the far end is used to store rolling stock awaiting repair, including in this view '*Topham*' which was built in 1922 by Bagnalls of Stafford. The signal post on the right was the down distant for Birchden Junction.

2018

Nature seems keen to reclaim a wagon awaiting its turn in the restoration queue.

When Class 207 demu 1317 first returned to the railway it was in excellent mechanical condition, having received an engine swap – perhaps the railway equivalent to a heart transplant – shortly before arrival. The same could not be said of its external appearance. However, such was the demand to have the unit in service it initially ran still wearing the patched up livery of Connex, its last operator. In a marked contrast to the appearance of 1317 today, it is seen climbing Birchden Bank.

37254 and 33063 bring a short engineers' train up Birchden Bank. The former up line remains, but is not connected to the engineers' siding. Little of the rolling stock on the railway is actually owned by the Spa Valley, the vast majority of locomotives and carriages are owned by individuals, groups, or independent societies, as noted by the small headboard. Note the tin shed, demoted from its previous role on Groombridge platform and now being used as a shelter for permanent way staff.

Tiny '*Martello*' appears to be bringing a five coach load up Birchden Bank with little effort. In reality it is being banked by a diesel unseen behind the trees.

Class 20 20118 awaits departure from Birchden. Before progress was made on re-opening to Eridge it was envisaged that a halt would be provided hereabouts; at one stage it was proposed to call it Harrisons Rocks after the adjacent sandstone outcrops.

Before the railway returned to Eridge, Birchden was the limit of operations and with trains tackling the bank from a standing start, spectacular departures could be guaranteed. 9466 and 47493 top and tail one such working.

Above
On 3rd September 2005 a special gala day was held to mark the naming of 33063 *'RJ Mitchell'* and its repainting into immaculate Railfreight Construction livery. After the ceremony it was put into service and is seen on Birchden Bank together with E6047 and 33065 on the rear of the train.

Right
Everyday work must go on; although a 2004 picture it's a scene straight from the 1970s or 1980s as a ballast working waits at Birchden with two BR blue Class 33s – 33065 and 33063.

DOGFISH

15224

Left
And on to Network Rail – Class 12 15224 propels a brake van through Birchden Junction onto the part of the line shared with London–Uckfield services. Birchden Junction signal box was behind the brake van. On the hillside is the house known as '*Glen Andred*'; built in 1867 in the 'Old English' style it set the benchmark for domestic architecture for some years after.
Above
Eridge remains an untouched Victorian gem of a country station. The shadow of the ornate 1880 iron canopy bracket is cast over a Southern Railway 'target' sign.

Running on the former up line, preserved Hastings demu 1001 passes Eridge signal box forming an Oxted–Uckfield working. The Spa Valley tracks can be seen waiting their new life on the right. Back in 1988 when BR accepted a deposit for the line between Birchden and Tunbridge Wells they also agreed that one track between Birchden and Eridge on the now singled Uckfield line, together with platform, buildings and infrastructure at Eridge, would be retained for heritage operation. Without this commitment, subsequently honoured for nearly 20 years by Railtrack and Network Rail, the railway you see today would not exist.

English Electric built diesel 50019 *'Ramilies'* undergoing restoration in the down bay platform.

The downside bay platform, sleeping in the summer sunshine, awaits the return of trains to Tunbridge Wells.

Return to steam at Eridge. The first steam locomotive back in over 40 years was a main line excursion to Uckfield, beating the Spa Valley by a couple of years. The locomotive was 'Black Five' 45407. Nevertheless, the Spa Valley 'side' of the station was thronged with wellwishers, including uniformed staff that had come to watch the train pass before the start of their duties at Tunbridge Wells.

Having been abandoned for over twenty years, nature took over the rails in platform 3 with a photogenic carpet of flowers. This display could not survive the refurbishment of the track which commenced shortly after this photograph was taken.

An historical curiosity is the mail chute beneath the footbridge steps. This allowed mail bags and other bulky items to be dropped from the station office at road level down to the platforms without the need for anyone to carry them down the short flight of stairs. Given the labour intensive nature of the Victorian railway, why this was provided at a relatively quiet country station remains a mystery. On the right new friction buffer stops mark the limit of Spa Valley operation on the former down line. We have come to the end of our journey.

Heralding the next chapter in the Spa Valley's existence – to be covered in a subsequent volume – 2008 saw contractors undertake the refurbishment of the former down line for heritage use. Vegetation has been cleared and, amongst a multitude of tasks, the truncated pointwork will be 'plain-lined'. On the adjacent track Turbostar 171804 forms a London Bridge–Uckfield working on the former up line. To the right is the 'long siding'.

Eridge signal box, built in 1880 and closed in 1991 appears to be disappearing into an autumnal woodland slumber. Compare the tree growth with that on page 18. Although retained for heritage use, its position on the opposite side of the national network line meant it could not immediately be reactivated to working use when the Spa Valley returned trains to Eridge. Its downstairs locking room did however shelter the lever frame from demolished Birchden Junction box until it could be reused in the new box at Groombridge.

After twenty five years and only five miles our journey is over. The Spa Valley train will return through the Weald to Tunbridge Wells. I hope you have enjoyed the trip and will return both to the railway itself and to a future volume charting the next few years of the railway's ongoing story.

SPA VALLEY RAILWAY
DO WELL · DOUBT NOT
NE · VILE · VELIS